EMPATHIC
SENSITIVITY

Books by Janice Carlin, Ph.D.

The Foundations System
Working with Multidimensional Energy
for Thriving

Be Free
Empowering Messages from The Light Book 1

Toward Ascension
Empowering Messages from The Light Book 2

Empathic Sensitivity
Powerful Tools for Coping and Thriving for
People Who Feel

EMPATHIC SENSITIVITY

Powerful Tools for Coping and Thriving for People Who Feel

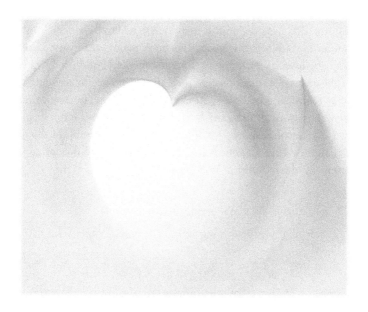

Janice Carlin, Ph.D.

Sacred Stories

PUBLISHING

Empathic Sensitivity:
Powerful Tools for Coping and Thriving for People Who Feel

Paperback ISBN: 978-1-945026-03-4
Electronic ISBN: 978-1-945026-04-1
Library of Congress Control Number: 2016903845

Published by:
Sacred Stories Publishing, LLC
Delray Beach, FL
www.sacredstoriespublishing.com

Printed in the United States of America

To the sensitive people of the world.

Remember who you are so that you may
do what you need in order to thrive.

ACKNOWLEDGMENTS

Thank you to my husband for going with the flow as we learned together about what it means to be an empath. Thank you to my son for being in my life and reminding me that there is more to reality than what I can see.

TABLE OF CONTENTS

INTRODUCTION

D o you feel and experience more physical and/or emotional pain than other people? If so, you very well may be an empath. You are not, however, a hypochondriac or a neurotic, crazy person because you feel so much unpleasantness. In this book, you will discover that your ability to feel so much is truly a gift that you can use to your advantage in your life to help yourself, and even others, if you so choose. You will learn ways to stop the cycles of pain that you experience and to move into a gentler and honoring way of living.

Being empathic is feeling energy sensitively. So in order to truly know what it is to be an empath and how to live a healthy, productive life as one, a knowledge base about sensitivity and how energy works in relation to yourself and the world is necessary. First and foremost, everything in our universe is made of energy. Science tells us that what we can see with our physical eyes comprises only 5 percent of all that actually exists. This leaves another 95 percent that we cannot see! What is happening on a non-physical, energetic level in terms of what you are experiencing relates to how you feel on an emotional or physical level.

In my book *The Foundations System*, I share a lot of information about energy, new science, and the interconnection of health conditions and sensitivity. If you would like a more in-depth explanation than what is presented here regarding these topics, you may want to read that book. Here, I will focus on the topic of empathic sensitivity and how you can live a healthy, productive life with your gifts.

This book is organized into four parts. In the first chapter, I describe what empathic sensitivity means, from a basic, traditional definition to a deeper, more authentic meaning. I share with you some of the concepts of energy, and explain how knowing about this empowers you to understand your gift on much deeper levels. When you have this knowledge, you can maintain your boundaries so much more easily. This leads to Chapter 2, which is all about boundaries. You will read about boundaries from a larger perspective than perhaps you may have heard before. In the third chapter, I share some valuable, accessible tools with you. These are tools that you can use on all levels in your life to bring about peace, grounding, and vitality for yourself. This can allow you to step into your power to use your gift of being empathic for the good of yourself, your family, and others in a safe and productive way. The final chapter illustrates some real-life examples so you can see how to apply all that you have read and learned.

For myself, knowing about being empathic and having effective tools to work with my gift was a crucial step in my own healing journey because it allowed for me to stop believing that there was something wrong with me. As I did, I was able to step away from feeling hopeless and helpless, and step into feeling empowered, strong, and capable. Before I understood what was really going on, I could not remain feeling stable, healthy, and grounded no matter how much I wanted to or how hard I tried. I learned over time that being grounded is a necessary part of feeling good and being healthy in life, but for me, as an empath, being able to do it would require some extra knowledge and tools. It brings me great joy to be sharing those here with you!

CHAPTER ONE

ABOUT EMPATHIC SENSITIVITY

Being an empath means that you can sense and feel the emotions and energy of others within yourself as if they are your own. This is different from being empathetic and feeling compassion toward someone else and what they are going through. As an empath, you can actually experience the emotions and/or physical pain of another, and it can be quite a confusing task to be able to tell what is your own and what is someone else's. Empaths can also feel the pain of animals and can even sense the pain and imbalance of planet Earth. You can sense the pain, but you can also sense the joy. It is a gift, not a curse. Remember this as you read through this book. If you do not already see it in this positive light, I think you will by the end.

Another word for empathic sensitivity is clairsentience, which means "clear-feeling." Empaths often can feel sudden moments of physical or emotional pain (grief, anger, fear, etc.), which seem to come out of nowhere.

When empathic people live without awareness of their sensitivity, they can experience many different, often undiagnosable ailments. They are often labeled as mentally ill, bipolar, depressed, hypochondriac, autistic, having chronic pain conditions, or ADD. Holding onto the energies of others can eventually lead to physical disease in empathic, sensitive people.

In order for me to take you deeper into a more authentic meaning of empathic sensitivity, you have to know some very basic concepts about how energy works and how you fit in with that. Having knowledge about energy and energetic boundaries is absolutely vital for empathic people to live in a thriving, healthy, happy state.

Energy exists in different forms and on multiple levels simultaneously. Energy, in its different forms, comprises our universe and everything in it. All of this energy is connected to itself; it is one thing—energy. We are connected to each other and to everything in our universe because of this energy. Essentially, we are the energy ourselves.

It's All About Vibrations

When I was in the midst of struggling with my health years ago, I kept asking, "Why is this happening? How is this happening? And if I can't understand it, how can I explain it to anyone else?" I kept hearing in my mind, "It's all about vibrations." As a classically trained musician and teacher, I'd had plenty of experience teaching about vibrations, but combining what I already knew with scientific information was something different. After many years of reading about quantum mechanics and doing my own channeling, I can tell you that it really is all about vibrations.

Science shows us that everything is made up of vibrations, which exist as patterns or waves. The simplest way to conceptualize vibrations is to think about the strings of a violin or guitar. When a string is plucked, it can be visibly seen moving back and forth rapidly, or vibrating. If part of the string is blocked from vibrating, by placing a finger upon it, the area of the string that is free to vibrate is made smaller. When plucked, this shorter area will vibrate at a faster rate, resulting in a higher-pitched sound. Plucking a string will also cause another string, which is an octave (eight tones) higher or lower than that pitch, to vibrate as well because it is vibrating in resonance to the first pitch, as they are directly harmonically related.

Each person has a unique vibrational signature that makes them who they are. Knowing this concept allows you to identify and use other energetic vibrations to support you in your highest good; that is, vibrations that are in harmony with your own. Energetic vibrations make up food and body products, colors and designs of clothing, friends and animals in your life, places that you go, and entertainment that you listen to or watch. You do not have to consciously know your vibration with your mind, but in reminding yourself that you have a unique vibration, you are acknowledging and honoring your true state of being. As you remember this, you are allowing yourself to step into a more authentic way of living. You will benefit from bringing to yourself vibrations that vibrate in harmony with your own.

This leads to harmony, which is the blending of vibrations into one complete, perfectly balanced whole. Harmony and dissonance describe the ways in which vibrations can exist together. To our ears, when two or more tones vibrate together in certain intervals (the distance between the tones), and the sound is nice and pleasing, they are said to be harmonious. When notes are combined in certain ways, they either produce harmonious sounds or the opposite: dissonant ones. The way our ears perceive sound in this way is important because it is a message to remember that vibration is everywhere and that some combinations of vibrations do not sound or feel good.

Your energy is innately highly vibrational. Although you are connected to everyone and everything, in that all is made of energy, some energies are low-vibrational; that is, they are toxic and harmful to your own energy. These toxic energies cause a dissonant or nonharmonic reaction when they come into contact with your own. This can manifest within you as pain and illness on any level. Remember that your body is a natural, organic vehicle in which you, your soul essence, live your life here on Earth. Essentially, these toxic energies are not from purely natural sources as you are. I share in more detail about these toxic energies further in the book.

The different forms of energy interact constantly in different ways and on multiple levels. Sometimes you can know what you are interacting with and sometimes you cannot. This is due to the concept of quantum entanglement. Entanglement shows that when pairs or groups of particles are entangled, they become entwined, communicating with each other, affecting each other, and correlating with each other without regard to the distance between them. Scientists have observed actual correlated physical properties between them. Albert Einstein called this "spooky action at a distance," because he did not really understand why it was happening—but it is not really spooky at all. It is just the way things work. The problem for people is that we cannot see these connections with our eyes to be able to know what is entangled with what or whom. But remember, we can only see about 5 percent of everything that exists. The lines of entanglement lie within the 95 percent that we cannot see.

As you interact with different energies, you experience something. These experiences of interaction occur on multiple levels within you. I will simplify this in terms of five basic levels: physical, mental, emotional, etheric, and spiritual. The mental level includes thoughts and beliefs; the emotional level includes emotions and emotional feelings; the physical level includes all that can be sensed with the five senses; the etheric level includes all energetic processes that occur outside of the realm of our five senses; and the spiritual level is the soul essence.

As you experience interactions of energy on these different levels, energy communicates with you. It is like a dance that is ever-evolving and changing in each moment to accommodate the dancers' every movement, sensation, and thought. The music shifts and tempos speed up and then slow down according to what is being communicated between the dancers. Even the backdrop of the room will change and their costumes will change as they change and interact with each other. It is intended to be a beautiful and graceful exchange of energy. However, because people have forgotten about how energy works and how all are interconnected with everything, the dance has turned into more of a street fight. Now, when interactions occur that do not feel good, we tend to reach for medications or call a doctor to try to get rid of them. When interactions occur that lead us in a different direction that might not make logical sense, we call a psychologist because surely we must be going crazy. Instead of this beautiful, interactive, communicative dance, we are roughly reacting, judging, doubting, and fighting off all that we do not like or desire to experience. However, there are much gentler, easier, and more effective ways to exist, some of which I share with you in this book.

If you understand pain as your energy systems' alert that something is dangerous to you in some way, you allow for so many more options to resolve the pain. If these messages are interpreted with presence and clarity of mind, you can see that when you feel pain, you can care for yourself either by removing yourself from a toxic situation or environment or by clearing lower vibrational energies away from you. The first step is simply to become aware that you are interacting with some kind of energy that is not in harmony with your own. Unfortunately, this is not what most people do. We have been conditioned to either ignore the pain or to worry, panic, and rush to a doctor or to the medicine cabinet for pain-killing medicine. Yet the pain is simply a message, which will continue to repeat itself in whatever way necessary until it is heard and resolved. The more that people change in their own lives and in our world to benefit the greater good of all, the less low-vibrational energies we are going to experience and feel as pain and illness. You have the power and the right to learn to reinterpret these messages and to change your conditioned reactions so that you can respond in different and more honoring ways.

The Authentic Definition of Empathic Sensitivity

With all of this in mind about energy, we can see a new definition of empathic sensitivity emerge. Empathic sensitivity is the gift of being able to clearly sense and feel the connections between ourselves and all of life and of energy in its multiple forms.

Unfortunately, the gift of empathic sensitivity has been extremely misunderstood. When an empathic child cries because her class is writing letters to soldiers in Iraq and she feels the loneliness, pain, despair, and violence that those soldiers and their families are feeling, she is told that she is "too sensitive," or "needs to have a thicker skin." People who are sensitive in this way to energy can feel the energies of other people and other things on many levels, including in their thoughts, emotions, and physical body. Empaths can walk past a grieving person and become overwhelmed with sadness or melancholy; they might begin to feel nauseous, afraid, or feel physical pain in their bodies. This does not deserve a diagnosis of depression, moodiness, hypochondria, or bipolar disorder. What is really happening is that they are reacting to fear-based energies and vibrations that are not their own, and they are becoming ungrounded. Many are taught that allowing oneself to feel and to be sensitive are negative, and this lesson is reinforced through educational systems, medical systems, social interactions, families, and in the work place. However, all that you need to do is to simply learn how to move the energy away that does not feel good, and to keep as much of it away from you as you can in the first place. Then you will have allowed yourself to live more authentically. You will feel peaceful acceptance of your gifts.

The gift of empathic sensitivity reminds us of the interconnections between ourselves and all of life. Vibrations are vibrations, and to many people, there is no difference between something that exists on the physical level and something that exists on another level, although it may be out of their cognitive awareness. Because we are all interconnected, an empathic person can sense toxicity nearby even when it is someone else who has eaten something containing a toxin. The empath will sense everything—from the disharmony that the ingestion of this food causes within the body, to the belief systems that the person holds, which have resulted in them making the choice to consume this product. If the empathic person is not aware and careful, she will experience it as if she ingested the toxin as well. She will sense the person's allergies and sensitivities as well as their reaction to the toxic substance. This is what is happening to the empathic children who are being diagnosed and medicated today. This is what has happened to many who live with chronic pain conditions in this world.

The goal is to move from reacting to interacting. When you interact, you can choose whether you want the energy near you or not. If it hurts and does not feel good, you can then choose to remove it from your space. This is gentler and more effective than attempting to treat yourself with medications or using any types of toxins such as sugar, nicotine, alcohol, self-judgment, or drugs. You can simply remove anything that you do not want from your space and continue on with your life. You will read about how to gently and effectively do this later in the book.

The most important message for you as an empath to hear and to know is that IT IS NOT YOURS. The pain that suddenly shoots through parts of your body, the tears that flow without warning, the mood changes that sneak up on you, the lack of ability to think clearly—these are reactions to energies on different levels. They are not you and they are not yours. When you can remember this, you can step out of helplessness and dependence on doctors and healers and into your own personal empowerment.

Knowing if you are truly an empath tells you something about your soul—your true essence. It gives insight and information about who you really are. Surely, you have noticed that not everyone is empathic. But the fact that you are does not mean that there is anything wrong with you—only that you are different from some people. And knowing who you are is a huge piece in being empowered to thrive.

Empaths' souls are sourced from spaces beyond humanity. In general, people do not use their intuitive senses to see and know beyond what they perceive in the physical world. On the outside, we all look like humans; on the inside, this is not what all of us are. At this time, otherworldly souls are incarnating on Earth to fulfill various missions that involve being of assistance to the souls already here and the planet that is being destroyed. When empaths use their gift with discernment, they can zero in on the elements that need to be changed so that the planet and the living beings upon it can finally heal.

Empaths feel energy that is beyond the third dimension. Knowing that this is what is going on results in your freedom to finally find peace within and be able to thrive.

CHAPTER TWO

BOUNDARIES

It is essential for empaths to maintain their boundaries with conscious awareness. As you will see when I discuss intuition later, empaths can feel energy that exists beyond the five senses, beyond mental thoughts, and beyond emotional feelings. Empaths can sense energies in all forms. So you have to be aware that your boundaries must be attended to on multiple levels.

Boundaries are kind of like putting up a fence around your yard to say, "This is my space. You are welcome to come into it **if you ask and I grant you permission to do so.**" The problem lies in that some energies do not respect this rule. It is because of this that you need to be diligent about maintaining your boundaries. Maintaining boundaries involves keeping toxic, low-vibrational energies out and away from you to the best of your ability.

The Multiple Levels of Toxic Energies

Below is a brief description of how the toxic energies that affect you exist on multiple levels. As the toxins exist on these multiple levels, so do your boundaries. This chapter examines each level in detail. They include:

Spiritual
The lack of strong boundaries and being un-present

Etheric
The disregard of intuition

Emotional
Violence, judgment, hatred, guilt, aggression, fear

Mental
Negative, limiting beliefs and the thoughts and perceptions they create

Physical
All chemicals, including additives, preservatives, medications, vaccines, GMOs, pesticides, herbicides, petrochemicals, chlorine and fluoride in water, and chemicals in cleaning and body products; heavy metals; sugar; tobacco; alcohol; drugs

Mental Level Boundaries

Thoughts are a product of the beliefs that you hold within yourself. When you hold negative, limiting beliefs about yourself and others, you can find yourself thinking negative, limiting thoughts. Beliefs also affect the ways in which you perceive the world around you. Perceptions define the reality in which you live. So, for example: If people have the belief that they are flawed and not good enough, then they will continue to think thoughts about how others are better and how they could never be as good-looking, or smart, or capable as them. Therefore, the reality of their life turns into situation after situation of experiencing themselves as "less than." This can take the form of never getting the promotion, the job they really want, the partner they would like to have, etc.

When you hold low-vibrational, toxic beliefs, then you will bring low-vibrational, toxic energies (experiences) to yourself. This imposes upon your own boundaries. For example, if you believe that you are inherently bad, then you will treat yourself in dishonoring ways. Essentially, you will find ways to bring dissonance to your own light, such as eating junk food or purposefully hurting yourself or others. Therefore, in order to maintain strong boundaries on a mental level, it is essential to get rid of these negative, limiting beliefs and to replace them with positive, empowering ones. When you change your beliefs, you change and shift your life, as you are then able to keep low-vibrational, toxic energies from entering your mental level boundaries.

Empaths can pick up on energies in all forms. Your energy systems and your body can translate the energies you pick up from another person or thing in different ways. Being in contact with fear-based, toxic energies may result in your feeling physical pain, or you may begin to feel angry or sad, or you may begin to think very negative thoughts. You may be entangled with energies that are beyond your awareness that are resulting in these unpleasant thoughts and feelings. Essentially, the vibrations of the energies can be translated into feelings, sensations, and thoughts in your mind.

The more low-vibrational beliefs you hold within yourself, the more negative energies will be attracted to and become entangled with the negative thoughts that were already being created from your beliefs. But sometimes, the thoughts just come through no matter what, just like the energies do through your physical body. So remain aware that if you are thinking negative thoughts and they do not resonate with what you believe, then all you need to do is to simply let them go and clear them away. Do not blame yourself for having thought them. There is low-vibrational energy all over the place on Earth right now, and your being is going to translate it into different forms. Just let it go and follow the instructions for clearing in Chapter 3. As long as you remember that this is what is really occurring, you can let go and they will not affect you adversely in the long term. This is how you shift from reacting to interacting.

When you find yourself suddenly thinking negative thoughts, say to yourself: "There is one of those negative thoughts again. I must have picked upon a low-vibrational energy. Oh well. I am happy that I can help the Earth and the beings that live upon it by clearing this energy away." Then, clear the energy (using tools you will find in Chapter 3) and move on with your life. Judging yourself or medicating yourself for having these thoughts is not serving you in your highest good. You have the power to stop negative energies, and once you get into the habit of doing so, they will become less prevalent for you. Stop them quickly, without analyzing, and move forward.

Physical Level Boundaries

In order to maintain your physical boundaries, it is necessary—to the best of your ability—to have the awareness of how to avoid bringing toxins into your body in the form of chemicals in foods, water, body products, and the air that you breathe. When you allow yourself to consume and to use toxic chemicals, you are breaking through your own protective boundaries.

In general, the toxic elements for all people are chemicals. Those found in foods and drinks include:

- Preservatives

- Additives (artificial colors and flavors)

- Artificial sweeteners

- Pesticides, insecticides, fungicides, and herbicides

- Genetically modified organisms or GMOs (non-organic soy, corn, canola, sugar, zucchini, and some potatoes, salmon, and apples)

- Petrochemicals (supplements and additives)

- Hormones, antibiotics, and medications given to animals (in milk, meat, and eggs)

- Chlorine and fluoride in water

I highly recommend removing all of these chemicals from your diet and then looking toward what else you may be reacting to in an allergic or sensitive way. Remember that grains are often treated with numerous chemicals and bleaches, especially when removed from their natural, whole form—so when you consume them, you are also consuming all of those chemicals. Also, many toxic chemicals are added to household cleaning products and body products, including cosmetics, soaps, shampoo, and lotions. Read labels carefully. If it is toxic to consume, it is toxic to put onto your skin. Refer to the Environmental Working Group's Skin Deep website (www.ewg.org/skindeep) for information about what is in the body products you use.

Beyond the chemicals, there are certain foods that make it more difficult to maintain your boundaries. Eating inflammatory foods such as gluten, sugar, and dairy, plus chemicals makes it more difficult to remain grounded and stable-feeling. The energy of these substances do not interact well with the human body and thus put extra strain on the immune system, taking away the energy needed to maintain strong boundaries. Sugar is a known toxin to the body and it is wise to avoid consuming it. Foods are different for different people. Find out what you are reacting to and make sure not to eat foods to which you are sensitive or allergic. In Chapter 3, you will learn tools for using your intuition to do this.

Additionally, medications and synthetic supplements are toxic. Sometimes there is a need; however, using these on a daily, consistent basis weakens the physical boundaries. I am not saying to stop taking your medications cold turkey right now, but simply to be aware that they are covering symptoms rather than addressing the issues at the root cause. If you are empathic, remember that the pain you feel is not because of you or even yours most of the time. Taking medication for someone else's pain is allowing your boundaries to be weakened. Something created within a laboratory is not going to resonate with the body in the same fashion as something natural, and will, in fact, cause dissonance.

Also, you can maintain your physical boundaries by not purposefully allowing into your space anything made of toxic chemicals that assault your senses. This includes perfumes and fragrances; loud, dissonant noises; and cigarette and cigar smoke. Of course, these are encountered throughout the day as you are out in the world, but it is your choice whether to stick around and let them invade your space, and it is your choice whether to purposefully bring them to yourself, such as by smoking or purchasing items with chemical fragrances added.

Vaccines are pushed, especially toward parents to give to children, and toward elderly people. The list of toxic ingredients in vaccines is really quite intense. Some of the ingredients include MSG (a neurotoxin), thimerosal (toxic mercury), formaldehyde, egg protein, aluminum (toxic metal), antibiotics, bacteria, viruses, and more. Remember that it takes only a miniscule amount of any substance to cause an allergic or sensitive reaction within an individual. The more different toxic elements are added together, the more amplified the toxic effects. This is called synergistic toxicity. You can choose what you will allow into your body and your children's. Having awareness of the ingredients allows for conscious decision-making. When you remain conscious and aware in your daily choices, you strengthen and reinforce your mental boundaries and all of the boundaries that your decisions impact.

Nourish yourself with nutrient-dense foods and keep toxins away from you—this will strengthen your immune system, which acts as the guardian of your physical boundary level. Vaccines, medications, and chemicals will only weaken it.

Your beliefs will impact your decisions to bring toxic elements into your body and your home. If you believe that something will not harm you because of an advertisement you have seen about it or simply because it is allowed to be sold in stores or online, then you are not living consciously. This is harmful to you and does not allow you to maintain your boundaries. These elements are toxic to the body and you will benefit from avoiding them completely:

- Alcohol

- Cigarettes, cigars

- Soft drinks—with sugar and sugar free

- Caffeine—coffee, tea, chocolate

- Recreational drugs

- Sugar

- Processed foods

- Chemicals

- GMOs (Genetically Modified Organisms)

Emotional Level Boundaries

As an empath, you have most likely had the experience of suddenly being overwhelmed by grief, anger, or fear. This is your energy picking up on fear-based energies; it is not mental illness or an anxiety attack coming from within you! The beliefs in fear and separation that people have created have resulted in great amounts of violence, illness, and pain on this planet. Just because you are not in the same physical space as a violent act or thought being created and put into action, that does not mean that you cannot sense or feel the energetic repercussions of it.

Imagine that everything is connected through a matrix of intersecting lines. Energy travels along these lines and across the spaces between them. As it travels, it interacts with other energies, including you. Like tiny messages of energy being carried along, the fearful, violent energies communicate with you. You do not have to react in pain or fear to them, however. As they come near you and you become aware of them, you can use some of the tools described in Chapter 3 not only to clear them away from you, but also to transmute them to higher vibrations so that they will cause no further harm. And please remember that, in actuality, there are not real lines. Everything is simply connected as one, big thing. What impacts one person will impact others who are entangled with them and the associated energies.

Many highly sensitive and empathic people of all ages can spend a lifetime in therapy wondering what is wrong with them because they cry so much. They suffer from what doctors can only call "hypochondria" because science can find no physical proof of any imbalances. Sensitive people seem to have no ability to have a "thicker skin." Until health professionals become aware of empathic sensitivity and how energy affects people on all levels, they will continue to misunderstand and mistreat empaths. Bipolar disorder, the emotional instability that accompanies autism and ADHD, depression, anxiety, and chronic pain and illness can be directly related to empathic people being unaware and not maintaining strong enough boundaries on all levels. Once you become aware of your gift and use tools to maintain your boundaries and to stay grounded, you will open the doors to allow your mental health conditions to resolve.

It is often difficult for empaths to sustain a feeling of inner peace. This is because we can so easily sense the violence in this world. The point remains not to judge yourself for this. If someone you know is able to feel peaceful and calm all of the time, good for him or her! If it feels good for you to be around them, to help you to connect to more peace, then by all means spend time with them. But do not judge yourself for feeling other emotions and sensations. You are alive on this planet and there is much discord here. Judging yourself for feeling the dissonance that definitely exists here does not make sense. Just because you have the gift of being able to feel does not mean that there is anything wrong with you. If everyone could and would allow themselves to feel as much as an empath does, there would be no choice but to clean up this planet and the pain that exists here immediately.

Etheric Level Boundaries

Experiences on this level are in the non-physical realm. You cannot touch them, but you can hear, see, and know them through your other intuitive senses of clear-hearing, clear-seeing, and clear-knowing, in addition to empathic clear-feeling. In order to maintain your etheric level boundaries, you must consistently use discernment in regards to your intuition. Make sure you are completely clear before channeling or asking for intuitive guidance. Ask where the information is coming from that you are receiving. The only information that you can trust, which is in your highest interest and for the highest good for all, is information from, with, and within The Light. Always use discernment as you develop and work with your intuitive skills.

There are many people out there who are saying a lot of things about spirituality and about energy. They call themselves "thought leaders." This is something to take very seriously. If someone is working from the level of thought and trying to convince you to believe something, then you must listen with a discerning ear. What they think is not the same as what is actually the truth. People start believing what famous people say and passing the word on to others. However, we are best served to ask where the information is coming from and if it is in the highest interest to pass it on. Always check in with your intuition on this level, beyond what you feel emotionally or physically, and definitely beyond what you believe or think to be true.

Additionally, be aware that many intuitive healers, energy healers, and practicing psychics are not taking the concepts of empathic sensitivity and entanglement into consideration when they relay information to you about yourself. You have to use your own discernment. If I had a dollar for every time I paid or listened to a healer tell me that I had more past lives to clear and heal, and more past experiences from this life to resolve, I would be a very rich person! The same issues would come up over and over in every session I had. For years and years, I paid people to "heal" them for me. This continued until I realized that these energies were not even mine at all. I was healing and clearing other people's stuff, and it was painful and awful for me to experience. Now that I have awareness of how energy works and how I react and interact with it, I am completely free from these experiences and I have not paid a healer in years.

Spiritual Level Boundaries

Pain and imbalances that are felt on other levels exist first on the spiritual level, or the level that cannot be seen, heard, or felt with our physical senses. Often they come into our awareness as thoughts first, and when ignored, they turn into physical or emotional pain. When you can address it here, you can avoid it manifesting into actual diseases and conditions. You will read more about how to do this in Chapter 3.

When you choose to be around people who make you feel badly about yourself, who do harmful and hurtful things to themselves and others, and who encourage you to dishonor yourself, you are allowing your boundaries to let down. When you purposefully choose to have toxic, hurtful people in your life, you are saying that you choose to let go of your boundaries and allow for yourself to be hurt. Remember that, because all is connected, when one hurts someone else, they are also hurting themselves.

The key to maintaining boundaries on the spiritual level is to keep in mind at all times that you are good and you are light, no matter what. When you can love yourself unconditionally, then you are on the right track. When you doubt or judge yourself as flawed or un-whole in any way, then you are not maintaining your spiritual boundaries. There is nothing wrong with your soul! It is a beautiful light; it is who you really are.

Using Your Gifts for Good

Lack of using your intuition can have a toxic effect. Being an empath is having the gift of clairsentience, or clear-feeling. Some empaths have other gifts, such as clair-cognizance (clear-knowing), clairvoyance (clear-seeing) and clairaudience (clear-hearing). These intuitive gifts allow for you to experience dimensions outside of just the third dimension, where you see and experience the physical reality. Clairsentience allows you to feel what cannot be sensed with your physical senses. When you receive a message through your empathic sense, it is your intuition's way of getting through to you. These are the messages of Spirit, and they are pure and they are real. When you think about eating something and feel sick or pain, this is a message not to eat it. When you ignore these messages, you are ignoring energy's communications to guide you in your highest good. Remember not to react to them out of fear. Yes, pain and nausea do not feel good, but if you just give yourself a moment and remain calm, you can resolve the feelings quickly. Listen to the communications. Although they do not come in the form of clear words or pictures for everyone, feelings and sensations are just as valid and important. In Chapter 3, I give you some tools to be able to access your clairsentience to receive answers to questions that you ask.

Within this clairsentience lays one of the true gifts of empathic sensitivity: Empaths can feel non-physical energy as if it is on the physical and emotional levels. Essentially, those random pains, aches, and emotional outbursts are the reactions to the energy that you are encountering on the etheric energy level. Many people cannot feel them at all. But because you, as an empath, can feel them, it is a blessing to everyone in your life when you do something about them. This does not involve medicating yourself or believing that there is anything at all wrong with you. Instead, you can tell others that the toxins they are creating and using on any level are indeed harmful, no matter what anyone (doctors, government agencies, Big Pharma, Big Ag, any commercial on television, etc.) has said to the contrary.

If you feel pain in any way because someone in your family has used a chemical fragrance on their own body, then tell them. This pain is not yours; you are feeling their reaction to the chemicals. You feel it because you are connected to them; you feel it because you are supposed to help them to see that they need to stop using this. Likewise, if you feel pain in your heart when your husband has come home from work and has eaten a fast food hamburger, there is nothing wrong with your heart. It is his heart that is suffering and you are the messenger. **The message is the pain, and you are supposed to deliver the message.**

The gift of being empathic is that you can help others. The gift of being empathic is that you are so aware of low-vibrational, toxic energies that you can work to clear them away and to help this planet and every living thing upon it to have fewer toxins around them. Being empathic is the reminder that we are all connected; being empathic is the reminder that what one does affects everyone else. When you attend to the messages you are receiving and take action, you are doing a great service to all. If you numb yourself and ignore these truths, you are actually doing a disservice to more than just yourself.

The Importance of Presence

On the non-physical, energetic level, the concept of presence is extremely important regarding boundaries and well-being for empaths. Being present is about fully showing up as yourself in the present moment; it is about being with your body and it is about connection. Being with your body means to have your energy be fully present in the here and now, where your body is located. If your body is in a class or a meeting and your mind is thinking of lying on a tropical beach somewhere, then you are not fully present with your body. If you are caught up in memories and feelings from the past or thinking about the future, then you are not fully present. We all have the capability to be away from our bodies, but just because we can do this, it does not mean that it is in our highest good to spend all of our time this way.

Being present is vitally more important than some may think, and here is why: The body is designed to be connected to the soul energy. If only part of the soul energy is present with the body, the body will not function to its ideal capability, and it will be left open to other energies. It is like leaving the front door to your house open when you leave for the day, and then to feel shocked and surprised when you come home and find your house has been vandalized and important things are missing and everything is a mess. You need to stay with your body and protect it. It has been given to you as a gift and your soul has chosen it.

When you are not fully present, your brilliance is not able to shine through. Think of all you want to be; know that, if you want it, you can be it! This is your light wanting to express itself. You can allow it to do so by showing up in your full presence, thus maintaining your energetic boundaries. Techniques for getting present are shared in the next chapter.

Your space is yours and you can choose what and whom you allow into it. Remind yourself that you are sovereign over your space. State clearly and firmly, with eyes open, "This is my space!" This is a clear definition of your boundaries.

Empaths are going to continue feeling low vibrations until everyone stops using and creating toxins and violence. In the meantime, there are many tools that you can use to help yourself to stay healthy, stable, and grounded, which you will read about in the next chapter.

Relationships and Empaths

There are two more pieces in regard to boundaries. They are awareness and acceptance as connected to relationships (and this includes the relationship you have with yourself).

Awareness

First, being aware as an empath allows you to bring a unique dynamic to any relationship, but especially to those to whom you are closest. I personally have set the intention that I will not feel intensely for anyone/anything that is not in the highest good. In other words, we do not have to feel everything all of the time! But in the case of my family, or for my own self-preservation, I do choose to use my empathic gifts as needed.

Before I was aware of my own gifts, I suffered constantly from emotional and physical pain. It would come on quite suddenly and often lead to actual illnesses. But now, I recognize these sudden painful experiences as clear messages. Case in point:

One day, I picked up my son from school. I had been feeling fine on the drive over to get him, but within about thirty seconds of him being in the car, I was overtaken with crushing chest pains and feelings of anxiety. There was absolutely nowhere to pull the car over. I did not have time to wonder what was going on with me, so I immediately asked him, "What's wrong?" He told me that he was extremely stressed and anxious about a standardized test that he would have to take the following day. I was afraid I would not be able to continue driving safely, and my son knows all about energy clearing, so I yelled to him in the back seat, "Get that fear off of you right now! It's hurting you and it's hurting me! Hurry!" He let go and cleared himself. My symptoms subsided immediately as he did.

Once we got home, we were able to have a discussion and deal with the issue at hand without all of that anxiety and fear around the situation. And of course, with my son being an empath as well, on top of everything, he was carrying around the other kids' anxieties and other negative energies from the day at school. But if I had not been in awareness, I would have thought I was either having a heart attack or anxiety attack. I would have blamed myself for having something wrong with me, when it had nothing—NOTHING—to do with me at all. And if I had gone that route and self-obsessed about it, I would not have been able to beneficially serve my son in resolving his own anxieties and his desire to clear other people's energies. Awareness is truly the key.

Acceptance

What about other kinds of relationships? After all, as empaths, we want to be of help to people we care about. But what about the people in our lives who are not interested in what we have to offer? This is where the maintenance of boundaries is so essential. If you reach your energy out to someone who is unwilling to receive it, you are not going to feel good. The energy of resistance is very painful and you are exposing yourself to it by trying to offer assistance when it is not welcome. It is like going into someone's home uninvited and insisting to stay there and help them tidy up. This does not make sense to do, and neither does doing it on a non-physical, energetic level.

There was a point in time when no one in my family supported me in the lifestyle changes I was making to help my son and myself to be healthy, nor through my career change from being a music teacher to an author and natural health practitioner. It was all too different from what they believed about how things were supposed to be in our family and in the world. I had to make a tough choice. Although it was clear to me what to do from an intuitive and intellectual level, emotionally, I struggled with choosing my own path of authenticity over remaining the way I used to be and having their support in my life. I had to reach a point of acceptance that my decision had to be non-contingent upon receiving any support from them in any way.

It is this acceptance that is so important to our own sense of well-being. Energetically, here is what kept happening. I continued to try to show them that I was worth supporting. "I am helping people, I am doing good in the world through the sharing of my books," I would think, and I believed that eventually my family would see that. But they did not. And yet, each morning I awoke believing that perhaps this could be the day—maybe I would get a friendly email or a phone call from one of them or maybe one of them would actually read one of my books. That did not happen. And the more I held onto trying to make it be so, the more pain and sadness I felt. I saw the value in these people, and I still do. I believed that, because they were so valuable, what they loved and supported must be valuable as well. You can see where this is going. It affected what I believed about myself. Eventually, I came to terms with the fact that not everyone is going to accept what I do and what I say. That is life. My family gave me a gift in helping me to work through those emotions and beliefs so that I could remember that all that was necessary was to accept myself.

Here are a few remembrances you can use in regards to acceptance:

1. No one is more valuable than anyone else.

2. Everyone is valuable.

3. You are worthy of all of the good possible, just because you exist.

4. You can only change you.

5. If someone does not want to change, leave him or her alone and stay out of his or her energy.

6. You do not have to feel the pain of someone else's resistance to transformation and awakening. If you do, you need to detach your energy from them.

7. Remember how amazing and valuable you are.

It can be a challenge to allow someone to follow the path of their own choosing. But truly, would you not want this for yourself? I chose my path and my family chose theirs. We were on different roads leading to realities that were completely different from each other. They made it consistently clear to me which road they had chosen. Now, it was my choice to remain on my path and stay within my reality of my own choosing. Each time I reached back to them, I stuck myself back on that road that led to a life of disconnection, pain, misery, and untruth for me. All that I was working so hard to manifest in my life was stunted because I refused to stay fully in my own space. By always reaching back to them, I was putting myself upon two paths at the same time. On one, I was healthy, happy, successful, and thriving. On the other, I was struggling, weak, unaware, sickly, and miserable. I had to commit—so I let them go. Energetically, I let them go and I made the commitment to my own life path. Now I did not have to suffer any longer, and the personal wounds I needed to heal could finally close in peace.

It is important to realize that when you energetically and emotionally let go of attachment to anyone or anything, you allow the energy to move. Then new possibilities can manifest. In my story, eventually, my father came around and actually asked for my assistance for healing when he was extremely ill. He started buying my books and being a wonderful support to me after that.

CHAPTER THREE

TOOLS

As an empath, your goals are to remain aware and to take action to keep low-vibrational, toxic energies away from yourself so that you can remain grounded. This will allow for you to feel healthy, energetic, and stabilized. When you are grounded, you are better equipped to deflect toxic energies from yourself without having them attach to or affect you so much—essentially, without getting knocked off of your balance point. For many empaths—and I know I am one of these—it does not take much to knock us over. So remaining grounded is essential. I address the concept of grounding in more detail in the next chapter.

The tools that you can use to be grounded can be utilized on all levels. Remember that a multi-level approach is the most effective for empaths. I once had a healer say to me, "Boy, when you get sick, it really is on all levels!" I thought it was like this for everyone, but apparently it is not.

The tools we can use are limitless. I am sharing with

you the ones that are useful and highly effective for me and my empathic son, including some I have learned from others and many that have been intuitively given to me to use and share.

Physical Tools

First and foremost, maintain a pure, clean diet. As discussed in the boundaries section, this is essential. Maintaining a diet of organic, pure, whole foods is the number one thing in creating vitality and allowing for grounding. Make sure to avoid alcohol, cigarettes, drugs, and chemicals of all kinds. You can use green juices and smoothies for detoxification of your body. Regarding specific diets, remember that each person has a unique vibration which, when coupled with their unique life experiences, results in different dietary needs. Some sensitive people do really well on a vegan diet, while others need to have some animal products. We cannot judge ourselves for our unique needs, which do change over time. Be prepared to change what you eat based upon your needs in the moment. In order to get the nutrition you need from the natural foods you eat, you have to listen closely to your body to be aware of what it does need.

Many empaths feel drawn toward vegetarianism and veganism because of their compassion and high sensitivity toward the suffering of animals. It is absolutely essential to know about nutrition when making the decision to be a vegetarian or vegan. I did not do this when I became vegan, twenty-six years ago. Along with so many other people in the same situation, I suffered severe consequences. Be aware of two vital pieces of information if you are vegan/vegetarian: First, the foods that are marketed as fake meats and cheeses are mostly highly processed soy and wheat. They are toxic to the body. Second, it is essential that you get enough Vitamin B12, a nutrient that is mostly found in animal products. If you are vegetarian and eat cheese, eggs, or fish, you will be getting B12 through your diet. If you are vegan, you will have to be diligent about bringing this vital nutrient to your body.

There are several other special diets that are popular today. Remember, you have to eat the way that your body personally needs you to. With that being said, damage to the gut occurs from toxic exposures, including poor diet, vaccines, and medications. With a damaged gut, your body cannot function in the way it was designed and therefore you cannot live to your highest potentials for thriving. The Specific Carbohydrate Diet and the Paleo Diet are good to use for healing the gut. I would not recommend following them indefinitely unless you or your child has a medical condition that warrants this. The raw vegan diet is great for losing weight and healing conditions in the body like cardiac blockages and diabetes. Again, unless you have a specific health condition that requires remaining strictly on these diets for many years, do not feel that you cannot eat other foods that your body needs, once your healing is complete. You can use all of the energetic tools available, but if your body has damage and cannot process the food you are eating properly, you are not going to feel good and will not be able to maintain vibrant health. I have researched and used all of these diets and more in healing my son and myself.

The body, when functioning properly, is designed to detoxify itself. Our world is in an extreme state right now where the air, water, and ground are extremely polluted. Add this to the levels of toxicity that we have to deal with daily through the ingestion of and exposure to chemical toxins, and we have a need for detoxification that is beyond what our bodies are naturally designed to do. It is necessary to support the body as it works to clear the toxins it encounters on a daily basis by providing it natural ways to detox such as Epsom salt baths, daily time outdoors in the sunshine and nature, and pure, green foods.

Remember that being an empath means that you have a special type of sensitivity or way of interacting with energy. Radiation from cell phones, computers, and other technological devices can be very disruptive to a sensitive person's energy. Therefore, make sure to use EMF protection for yourself. This can be in the form of a pendant or crystal, which you can find on the Internet. Use the one that works the best for you. I personally use an apache tear obsidian crystal or tourmaline crystal that has been specially programmed. I also have a lot of crystals like obsidian around the Wi-Fi and cable boxes in my home to defray some of the EMF energy.

Some other tools you can use include:

- Make sure to get yourself outside every day. Avoid spending a lot of time in densely crowded and enclosed places. Open windows when you can. Get out in the fresh air when you can.

- Use earplugs if you need them. Do not be afraid or embarrassed to do this. This cuts out the extra audible energies so you can focus on remaining grounded and processing the other energies that you encounter.

- Use your intuition when it comes to eating. You will read more about this in the spiritual tools section.

If you smoke, drink alcohol, or use drugs, consider the effects that these toxic substances have on your ability to be grounded. They harm your body and damage your brain. Although they may provide temporary feelings of relief to you from the bombardment of low-vibrational energies you are sensing, their toxic effects upon your body actually make it more difficult for you to remain present and be grounded. Stopping yourself from being grounded is perhaps the most detrimental thing that you as an empathic person can do to yourself. Your soul energy cannot remain fully present within a body that is constantly ingesting toxins. Using alcohol and drugs to escape only sends a stronger message that your light is not welcome within your body. This is dangerous on more levels than most people talk about. Entities and negative energies can attach to you and harm you when you use these substances. Please take care of your body so that your true essence can be connected and grounded with it.

Mental Tools

Your mental tools involve remaining conscious and aware. Here are some things to keep in mind:

Expose yourself to the highest vibrational entertainment you can. When you watch television, movies, or things on the Internet, keep it light, loving, and humorous. Empaths can so easily tune into the emotions and thoughts of others that they can literally become ill when watching negative news in the media or violence in movies and on television. This includes books, magazines, and newspapers as well.

Stay conscious and do not buy into advertising. This is really important. For many people, ads are all around. You have to remain in a conscious state, using your discernment to make sure that you do not buy into believing something that simply is not true. Remember that what works for one person will not work for everyone. There is no right way to be. Healing in particular is different for empaths. This is why I developed a new healing system called The Foundations Healing System. You have to find what works for you. Do your best to avoid watching commercials as they try to convince you that you need to eat unhealthy foods or take medications to feel better because you have some kind of condition. Avoid looking at magazines that cause you to feel less than someone else in any way. Judging yourself is toxic to your energy in the same way as when someone else is judging you. Feed your mind the highest vibrational things you can. What you read, watch, and listen to can nourish your mind or have the opposite effect.

Letting go of limiting, negative beliefs and replacing them with empowering, positive ones is extremely important for healing and being healthy. In the section about Etheric and Spiritual Tools, you will find a technique that you can use. I encourage you to find the ways that work the best for you to shift your beliefs.

Emotional Tools

First and foremost, remember that when you are feeling emotions that do not feel good to you, they probably are not yours. They could be caused by an allergic or sensitive reaction to something you have ingested, smelled, or come into contact with, or to another person's negative emotions, thoughts, or actions. Consider this first. In order to stay grounded, you have to remember this. If you go straight into judging yourself or your children as being emotionally unstable and having some kind of condition or disorder related to that, then you are giving the energies—which really have nothing to do with you at all—a lot of power. You are essentially inviting them to stay, as you have taken ownership of them. So immediately say, "This is not mine!" Then allow it to go where it belongs in the highest good. Asking your Guides to assist is a good way to keep your energy from getting any further entangled. You can say, "My Guides, please clear this where it belongs in the highest good in the way of the highest good." That is it. Do not own it as your own.

Toxic energies hurt. They cause pain, disease, death, suffering, and illness. It makes sense that an empath who comes into contact with them will feel pain on some level. On the emotional level, it can take the form of crying, screaming, yelling, anger, fear, grief, depression, or violent behavior. Acknowledge that it is not yours. You are not violent, angry, or sad. The energy hurts. You are feeling the pain, you are sensing the pain, and you are crying because it is so toxic and so low-vibrational, and it hurts. You are crying because you feel the pain of others. It is not you and it is not yours. Do not own it for one second. Let it go.

Etheric and Spiritual Tools

This is where you will get into working directly on the subtle energy level. It is essential for empaths to learn to do this. In order to be grounded, you have to clear away the toxic energies from yourself. If you are keeping your body clean and clear from chemicals and maintaining a good balance of nutrients, and you are still hurting, it is because you have not addressed detoxification from a subtle energy level. I have combined the two levels here because energy healing really occurs on the spiritual level, while the use of your intuition through hearing, seeing, and knowing occurs on the etheric level. You will use all of this as you work directly with energy and The Light for healing and transmuting energies.

White Light

As an empath, you experience energies from multiple dimensions all the time. Therefore, you are going to use energies on the subtle level to your benefit. You can surround and fill yourself and the energy field that surrounds your body with pure, white light for the purpose of clearing, healing, rejuvenation, and even protection. Every morning and night, I ask the highest source—from with and within The Light—to surround me and my energy field with pure, white light and whatever colors I need in my highest good for keeping all low vibrations, entity and energy attachments, and everything not from The Light away from me, in the highest good. I ask to have the colors that I need in my highest good, because I do not know what they are in each moment, nor do I want to spend time figuring it out all day long. Intend for this light to remain there all day and night. Then, do it again in the morning.

Getting Present

The concept of being present is vitally important for empaths. Sometimes being present simply means to sit and to breathe and allow yourself to be. The most important thing to remember is not to judge yourself for not being present in any given moment, but to simply bring yourself back to being present. Being present is also about respecting the boundaries of others. It is important to connect with people; however, connection does not mean attachment. You cannot keep your energy attached to other people, places, or things and expect to feel great. Remember this, too, when you are feeling unpleasant things, because someone could be hooking themselves into your energy without you even knowing it.

Here is a visualization you can use to conceptualize being present:

Imagine you are a spider sitting in the middle of a web that you have created. The threads of the web consist of energy from yourself, for you have created them from your own energy. You have sent out these threads of energy away from your center for different reasons. Each thread connects on one end to you and the other end to another space away from you, be it of a person, a place, an object, an idea, or a thought. As these threads of your own energy connect to other energies, both you and the energies you have connected to are affected by this connection. As your energy interacts with other vibrations, your vibration will move, adapt, and change to maintain as much harmony and balance as possible within yourself. When you are finished thinking about or interacting with whatever energies you have connected to, it is important to let go of them. This will allow your own energetic vibration to remain stable and harmonious. If you do not let go, you will constantly be affected by these other energies, and your energy will have to constantly work to adapt to maintain balance within itself.

When you leave your energy connected to another person, you are tuned into their energy. Therefore, if that person is sick and you leave your energy connected to them, you are tuning your own vibration to that illness or allergy. When you remain attached, you are exposing yourself to all sorts of vibrations that are not your own, in addition to exposing that person to yours as well. Therefore, letting go and remembering not to attach to anyone or anything is of the utmost importance to both parties' well-being. Refraining from attaching your energy to that of others is a gesture of great respect toward them, as well as toward yourself.

Techniques for Getting Present

This is about getting your energy off of others while bringing it into your physical space. Remember that spider web? To get present, open up the ends of those threads that are holding onto other people, thoughts, or things and let go, returning that which is not yours to where it belongs, in the highest good. You can imagine that the threads are like little hands that are gripped closed. All you need to do is allow them to open. You do this by simply intending to do so. You do not have to know where it is going at all. Just let go. You can also ask your Guides for assistance with this process.

One of the problems with being un-present and attaching your energy onto others is that, when you decide to bring your energy back to you, you may also bring some toxic energies with it. Clear and heal your energy that has been away from you before you bring it back present. You can do this with intention and using the white light. Renowned psychic teachers, Esther and Jerry Hicks, once shared from the part of The Light they call Abraham:

We are all Vibrational Beings. You're like a receiving mechanism that when you set your tuner to the station, you're going to hear what's playing. Whatever you are focused upon is the way you set your tuner, and when you focus there for as little as seventeen seconds, you activate that vibration within you. Once you activate a vibration within you, Law of Attraction begins responding to that vibration, and you're off and running—whether it's something wanted or unwanted.[1]

With the intention to clear your energy that is away from your physical body, hold the image of pure, white light in your mind for seventeen seconds. The effects are more efficient if you can also maintain a feeling or sense of gratitude at the same time. Then, bring your energy back to where your physical body is. Just say, "I bring my energy back to myself for integration and grounding with my physical body in my highest good." Breathe and wait as you allow this to occur.

More techniques for clearing energy will be covered later in this chapter. Here are some other things you can do help yourself to be present during the day:

1. When you are having a conversation with someone, look them in the eyes or at least at their face.

2. Keep the television turned off in the house during meals and any time that is not designated as TV-watching time, so that you can focus upon the task you are doing in the moment.

---

[1] Quote from Abraham-Hicks, excerpted from the workshop in North Lost Angeles, CA, on August 18, 2002. http://www.abraham-hicks.com/lawofattractionsource/

3. Whenever you find yourself thinking of the past, future, or of someone else, gently tell yourself to come back to the present moment.

4. Honor yourself and listen. If you need to take a break and have some quiet time to yourself, then do that.

5. Sit quietly and focus upon feeling your body fully in the space where it is. Feel yourself sitting in the chair with your feet on the ground. Feel your back touching the back of the chair and your hands and arms on the sides. Rest your head against the back of the chair and know that you are fully supported in your body, right here and now.

6. If you feel that you have become very un-present and cannot seem to stabilize and feel grounded, try this simple yet effective exercise, which is telling yourself where you are. It is like sending out a homing signal to your soul energy. State, "I am on planet Earth." State the date. Then, go through naming where you are, starting with the big and working in with more detail. State the country, state/province, city or town, and street address. State exactly where you physically are. For example, "I am in my living room, sitting on the couch, holding a pillow. My feet are on the ground and I am breathing. I know

where I am. I am connected to my body and I feel good being here. I am present and grounded with my body right here and now." This is a great exercise for children to do for themselves.

In summary, always come back to being present. This is something that you can do many, many times throughout your day. Being present is about really consciously showing up as yourself in the moment

Clearing Energy and Being Clean

Being clear is about establishing clear personal boundaries for yourself. Different energies can attach to your energy in the same manner that you can attach to them. The process of clearing is simply about removing from your space all energies that are not yours/you, that have attached to you, and that are of low vibration.

Clearing energy on the non-physical level is simpler than a strong, physical detoxification protocol. Working with energy on the non-physical level involves a great amount of trust and faith. You can be assured that that what you are doing is not only highly effective for yourself, but beneficial to all as well. Working with intention on this energetic level means that manifestations will occur instantaneously there. So when you intend to clear your energy or a space, you will.

Imagine that your cells are filled with white light. As energies—including toxins from the environment, negative emotions, and energy attachments—accumulate in your energy field, the degree of light within your cells becomes denser. So instead of white light-filled cells, you have smoggy-looking, grey-filled cells—like air that has been polluted. The cleaner the air is, the better you can breathe and the healthier you will be. The same is true for your cells and for your energy field. So when your light-filled energy field that surrounds your body becomes polluted and negative energy-laden, you feel heavier, more burdened, less vibrant, and more ill. Children can keep going in a state of thriving health for only so long until they start to feel the density of polluted cells and energy fields as well. You can come into your life this way through the toxins you carry within your DNA and energetically through your ancestral lines.

Clearing your entire system is imperative to maintaining healthy cells and the healthy life-force energy within you. Messages that your body will send to you, to tell you that need to urgently clear, include sudden aches, pains, discomforts, yawning, fatigue, and mood changes. You can alleviate these quickly by clearing so that they will not get stuck and manifest into more serious dis-ease later. When you become aware of anything that just does not feel harmonious with yourself, this is a message to clear.

It is important to clear not only when you feel something unpleasant. Just as you must clean your dishes every time after you eat, wash your hands when they are dirty, and put away things after you use them so that your home is neat and picked up, you must also clean your own energy throughout the day. Sometimes cleaning your energy can be a quick and simple process, as compared to washing your hands before eating. Sometimes it can take more time and focus, like mopping the floors. No matter what you do, dust and dirt build up inside of your home and you must vacuum and clean it. The same is true for your body and your energy field. If you maintain a clean and clear state daily, then there is less to detoxify and clean out later on. It is like vacuuming your house every day. It takes some time and effort, but it feels so much better and lighter to live in. Just as you open the windows to bring fresh air into your home, and to air out stagnant and toxic air, you need to purify your own energy systems. When you do this consistently, there is never time for much unwanted energy to build up.

Clearing can sometimes be more complicated than getting present, because you are essentially removing other's energies from your energy field. Remember to be firm and insistent upon their leaving. Remind yourself that no one and nothing is allowed to attach to your energy field at all, because this is your space. Nothing can attach or come in without your permission. This is why it is so important to be and to remain present, so that you can be aware of when energies do entangle with and come into your space. Here is the gift of being an empath—you can feel when this happens, while other people cannot. Get present first, and then clear your energy in full. Techniques for clearing are included later in this chapter.

The Importance of Clearing After Releasing Energy

The mistake that many people make is that they let go of or release low-vibrational energies, but they do not clear them away. When they are allowed to be transmuted and cleared to where they belong, in the highest good, it assures that they do not remain within your energy field, body, or home, and they are not transferred onto someone else to whom they do not belong. Letting go, but not clearing, is akin to walking around like the Charlie Brown character, Pigpen, with a constant cloud of dirt around yourself. All you need to do is to remain in awareness with your conscious mind that you are intending to clear away all energies, which you release, directly where they belong in the highest good. From yoga and exercise, whether done individually or in a group, to massage, different therapies, energy healing, acupuncture, and even surgical procedures, whenever energy is released, it must be cleared away. It is up to you to do it. This clearing is for the benefit of the individual as well as the healer, therapist, or doctor. In a way, your energy systems can act like sponges. You need to be diligent about keeping them clear from lower vibrations.

Toxins and Being Clear

Energy can be cleared on the subtle level by anyone, even children. However, it becomes easier when you are already doing what is in your power to keep toxins away from yourself. When you remove as many toxins as possible from your life, you significantly lesson the load that your body and energy systems have to deal with on a daily basis. A constant stream of toxic bombardments to the body will overtax the immune system and result in illness, imbalance, pain, and discomfort. Some of the ways in which these can manifest on various levels include: Cognitive, in the ability to think and process information clearly, maintain focus, and concentrate; emotional, in the capacity to remain calm and centered; and physical, in the capacity to maintain physical health. Essentially, these low-vibrational, toxic energies can throw you off from your natural state of balance and homeostasis. Doctors and therapists have a lot of different words and labels to describe the symptoms that people experience when imbalance occurs. From a different perspective, it is all one experience of imbalance, due to the reaction (irritation and inflammation) to toxins.

Energy that cannot be seen with your physical eyes has the capacity to result in your experience of sickness, fatigue, emotional instability, and even nightmares. If this energy is not cleared away, the effects can lead to actual disease. Coupled with the onslaught of physical toxins, it is clear why so many people suffer with so many destructive diseases and health conditions. It is this lack of awareness in how we interact with energy that we cannot see and how toxins affect us that has led to the overwhelming amount of chronic pain and disease that exists today.

Be sure to remove the toxins on all levels that were referred to in Chapter 2. With the toxic load lessened on the physical level, there is less for your body to detoxify, and you can work with clearing energy on the non-physical level to maintain your health and balance throughout the day and night.

There are techniques that you can use if you were exposed to dishonoring abuse during your life. You can clear the low vibrations away from yourself, including all ill effects of the experience. You do not have to be doomed to live with the negative effects of a traumatic experience for your entire life. This is another belief that has led to physical, mental, and emotional pain and illness. There are many ways to transmute and clear these energies, some of which include EMDR, cognitive restructuring, hypno-analysis, or pure energy techniques, which I share in *The Foundations System.*

Boundaries and Clearing

In order to clear your energy, you have to establish clear personal boundaries. Remember that any lower vibrations you witness, feel, or experience are not who you truly are.

Remember also that your energy is of The Light and that the lower vibrations of pain and toxicity present near you (or anywhere on Earth) are not who you really are. Therefore, you do not need to accept them as part of yourself. Beliefs in fear, lack, and superiority have been passed to all of us from previous generations, and they are not intrinsically who we are. These beliefs have led people to create so much toxicity and violence on this planet already. These beliefs act as toxins themselves, which reside on the mental level. When you remember that they actually are not accurate—because anything of a low vibration is not authentic to who you really are—then you can step away from them and begin creating higher vibrational beliefs resulting in experiences and products that benefit yourself and others. As you are already intrinsically light, remember that when you clear, you are sending anything that is not light away from you, so that you can return to your high vibrational state of balance and harmony. You will find an effective technique for transmuting and clearing your own negative and limiting beliefs later in this chapter.

Clearing on the Non-Physical Level

In the highest integrity, I am sharing just the very basics of clearing energy here. There are many different techniques for clearing that are available. You can find what works the best for you. Methods for clearing on deeper levels—and the ways to align to the physical, emotional, and mental levels for quick and efficient clearing and manifestation—are provided in detail in *The Foundations System*, which is the complete version of the healing system I developed for highly sensitive people. It is available through Amazon.

No matter what method or techniques are used for clearing, there are four important concepts to remember:

1

First, it is important to surround yourself with pure, white light when doing clearing work. The white light is a purely positive energy, which protects you from lower energetic vibrations that may be attracted to the ones that are being released and cleared. Any time you become aware of negative energy around yourself, you can simply call forth this pure, white light to surround you. On this level, what you intend will instantaneously be so. Healers who do any type of work that involves them entering another person's energy field, releasing a lot of old energy, or anything that will lead to an out-of-body experience need to make sure to use the pure, white light for themselves, as well as telling the client/patient to do the same for themselves. Examples of when this is necessary include: psychic readings, hypnosis, psychotherapy, acupuncture, medical surgery, chiropractic, physical and occupational therapy, and physical examinations and procedures. In doing so, the healer shows respect for the client/patient's energy, as well as his or her own.

2

You are clearing away from your entire space, on all levels, all that is not yours and all energies and entities that have attached themselves to you. When you clear, you are doing a service not only to yourself. Make sure to intend that the energies be sent to exactly where they need to go in the very highest good. It may be that they go back to where they came from or that they get transmuted back into light. Some people become very concerned and interested in the details of what kinds of energies have attached themselves. This is due, in large part, to upbringing with Western medicine and Newtonian science, and the labels and delegations it provides for every detail. However, it is not necessary to know what they are or where they are going. You just have to let them go. They are not yours and they do not belong with you. In fact, the more attention that you pay to them, the more energy you feed into them.

3

After clearing yourself, it is extremely important to re-member to seal and repair your energy field, as some energetic attachments can cause damage to the field. I explain more about this and provide techniques for doing so below.

4

You can call on the assistance of The Light in whatever way you choose. If you intuitively sense any darkness and you feel frightened, remember that you do not have to do any of this alone. You can call upon Angels, your Guides, or Archangel Michael. Michael is the protector, and he will cut away cords of attachments and clear the lower energies away where they belong in the highest good. Simply call his name, silently or aloud, and ask for his help in clearing.

Basic Clearing Techniques

The following are three basic clearing techniques, followed by a more detailed technique for clearing stubborn attachments and the essential final step of sealing the energy field.

Clearing Technique Number 1:
Intention and Using White Light

This clearing technique works directly with manifestation and the Law of Attraction. In order to create what you want quickly, you have to know that it has already occurred. You must know what that feels and looks like to you. When your energy is clear, you will feel balanced and healthy, as well as any other feelings of peace or joy that you want to feel. Therefore, begin with a feeling of gratitude in your heart space. Just allow your heart to relax and fill with gratitude. The visualization you will use in this technique is pure, white light, because ideally you are returning to a state where this is what you are.

Have and hold the intention to be clear on all levels of all energies and attachments that are not yours and not of The Light. You can state this out loud or simply inside of your mind. Visualize white light around yourself and throughout yourself and hold the intention to be clear. If you can visualize a large circle or oval around your body that extends outward at least two feet all around and is filled with pure, white light, then this can be very helpful. Hold your visualization of the pure, white light along with a feeling of gratitude and the *knowing* that you are clear as you breathe for seventeen seconds. Once you have reached this time, state, "It is so." This technique is also highly effective for clearing objects, food, water, and space, such as your home. It is really this simple. Here are some more techniques that you can use, which are effective and helpful.

Clearing Technique Number 2:
Using a Clearing Vortex

Imagine a swirling vortex spinning to the LEFT, counter-clockwise. Place it on your body wherever you feel you need extra clearing. You can place one around your entire body, as well, with the top opening above your head like a funnel that is immediately clearing and transmuting energies to light. Intend that as it swirls, it is pulling out lower-vibrational energies and releasing them away from your body and your energy field, and they are they transmuted into the highest vibrations of light. Let it open up as a cone shape, away from you above your head.

Clearing Technique Number 3:
Vacuuming with Archangel Michael

This is a method that Doreen Virtue, Ph.D. teaches in her book Angel Medicine. You will work directly with this angelic being to clear yourself.

Ask Michael to place the vacuum tube in through the top of your head. You can adjust the suction speed by asking.

Next, simply follow the vacuum with visualization and intent as it moves downward throughout your entire body. You may be aware of darkness or blackness being cleared away. Doreen states, "Notice any areas of darkness, and work with Michael to direct the vacuum tube to these areas to suction the lower energies away." Remember to vacuum all of the organs, the spinal column, and down the arms and legs into the fingers and toes.

Doreen states:

Once the body is completely cleared, Michael will reverse the switch on the vacuum. Now, toothpaste-like liquid white light emerges from the vacuum tube, sparkling like diamond-white caulking material. It fills up the entire body, and heals and balances any former areas of distress. We thank Archangel Michael and his band of mercy angels for this healing and clearing. Saying thank you is a respectful return of positive energy to those who help us, be they in physical or in spirit form.[2]

Saying thank you is a respectful return of positive energy to those who help us, be they in physical or

---

[2] Virtue, Doreen Ph.D., Angel Medicine. (Hay House, Inc. 2004): p. 234

in spirit form. It is not necessary to be a completely clairvoyant person in order to use this method. Trust that you can see the dark stuff and trust that it is being removed. You do not have to know what it is; just let go and trust. You are safe and you are in the hands of a beautiful, loving, and powerful light being who only wants to help you. You may feel changes and shifts during the process, which is a good thing!

It is not necessary to be a completely clairvoyant person in order to use this method. Trust that you can see the dark stuff and trust that it is being removed. You do not have to know what it is; just let go and trust. You are safe and you are in the hands of a beautiful, loving, and powerful light being who only wants to help you. You may feel changes and shifts during the process, which is a good thing!

About Clearing Entity and Energy Attachments

Different energies can attach to your own energy. You can witness this in the physical world through parasites, whether they are microscopic entities or people who seem to hook into your energy and leave you feeling drained. When you clear yourself, you will be clearing these energies, plus any non-physical entities and energies that have taken up residence within your space. If an energy/

entity has attached itself to you, it is not from, with, and within The Light. Angels or light beings will never attach themselves to you—so if you are hearing, seeing, or feeling them conveying to you that they are from The Light, and they are attached, know that this is simply not true. The lower vibrations have a way of using persuasion and dishonesty (think of advertising, marketing, politicians) to get what they want, which is to attach to your energy. They drain your energy to use for their own purposes.

It is important to remember that your energy field is not designed to hold lower, negative vibrations and toxins within it naturally. Therefore, if you are holding these, then sometimes there are extra energies attached to them that are making it possible for them to remain with you. It is like you have made a deal or have a contract with these energies to do this for you so that you can experience the energies and vibrations, which are not yours and are not yourself. In the case that this has occurred, you will know, because you will find it difficult to be completely cleared within a few moments. Sometimes, you may intuitively know that an energy or entity has attached itself to you.

It is important to note that there is nothing to be afraid of regarding entity attachments. The bigger the deal that you make out of them, in terms of being afraid, the more this fear energy feeds them and adds more energy to them. Simply and firmly command them to leave and clear them away. If there happens to be a stubborn one, simply ask for help from The Light and Archangel Michael and non-physical Angels. Avoid any conversations with the attachment as you continue to firmly command it to leave. Continue to remember that you are light and that nothing has the right or permission to drain away any of your power or energy by attaching itself to you. You really have to be assertive with them.

Regardless of your religious beliefs, the group of light beings who assists with clearing are the Angels. You can call upon them at any time for help with this or anything else in your life. As you will see below, when clearing attachments, you will work with them so that your energy remains unharmed, and to ensure that all work is done in the absolute highest benefit of all. It is of a higher integrity to call up non-incarnated Angels, as Incarnated Angels can tend to quickly become un-present by sending their energy outward to be of assistance when they become aware of a call for help.

Remember that there are no prerequisites for having the ability to clear attachments. Anyone can do it!

Techniques for Clearing Entity and Energy Attachments

- First, make sure that you are present and have the white light in place around yourself, your physical location, and anyone around you in that space.

- State, firmly but respectfully, "I command all entity and energy attachments on all levels of my being to leave now, and to go directly where they belong in the highest good, in the way of the highest good. If they are unable or unwilling to leave on their own, then I ask the highest source from, with, and within The Light to take them now." Ignore anything that sounds or looks negative. These are the lower vibrations. Simply do not listen and remain diligent on letting go.

- State, "I ask my Guides to cut the ties of entanglements to anyone and anything on all levels of my being and to clear them away directly where they belong, in the highest good, in the way of the highest good, including the entities, energies, and vibrations attached to and associated with them."

- Do the basic clearing technique above, which is holding your entire self in the pure, white light for seventeen seconds, with the intent to clear, feeling gratitude and *knowing that it is so*. State, "It is so," when complete. Notice that there were two steps here. The first was to release and let go; the second was to clear. This is the part that is often overlooked, but is vitally important to include.

The Important Final Step!

Here is another piece that is often overlooked in clearing techniques, but is also important not to leave out. After clearing, make sure to seal and repair any rips, tears, and/or holes in your energy field. If you leave this step out, you are exposing yourself to lower vibrations that can cause more harm. You do not have to even know if there are rips or tears; you only have to intend that they be sealed and repaired. Do this step—no matter what—after any clearing work. To do this, simply state: "I seal and repair all rips, tears, and holes in my energy field, in my highest good." You can visualize this or just breathe and wait and know that it is so. State, "It is so," to complete.

Technique for Transforming Your Beliefs

Have a sheet of paper and pen or pencil ready. Close your eyes and take some very deep breaths. Allow your energy to be fully present with your body in the here and now through intention. Ask of your Higher Self and Guides, "What are the negative, limiting beliefs that I am holding that are not honoring of who I really am and are blocking me from living my life as a full expression of my authentic, vibrant, healthy self?" Listen and allow for the beliefs to surface. Write them down. For every limiting belief you write, be sure to write an empowering one to take its place. (You can do this afterward or simultaneously.) Get as many out as you can, and do not worry if you need another piece of paper to write more. Be aware that you may need to do this process again at a later time(s) because it may not be in your highest good to release and replace all of them at the same time. Do not judge yourself for the amount of beliefs, just keep writing them down and replacing them.

Here are some examples of positive, empowering beliefs, just for your reference as you choose your own:

- I am perfect for exactly who I am.

- I am powerful.

- I am gentle.

- I am peaceful.

- I am supported by The Light.

- I am guided only by The Light.

- I know what to do for myself to be healthy and thriving.

After you have finished writing, follow these instructions:

The low vibrations connected with the negative beliefs have to be cleared and transmuted. The work you have done is important and you will want to make sure that it is really effective. Here is how you can appropriately work with energy to ground the transformations and clear the low vibrations away for good.

Breathe deeply and make sure that your energy is fully present with your physical body in the here and now where you are. Once you are sure that you are present, call upon your Higher Self and Guides. You can do this by saying, "My Higher Self and Guides, please come and help me now, in my highest good." Breathe deeply and intend to release all of the negative, limiting beliefs that you have written down. You can do this by saying, "I release all of the negative, low-vibrational, limiting beliefs I have written down. I also release all low-vibrational energies, entities, and contracts associated with and attached to them. I ask for all of these to be cleared directly where they belong, in the highest good now, in the way of the highest good." As you do this, continue to breathe. Allow for your Guides and Higher Self to help you to release and to clear the energies. They do not serve you in living to your highest degree of vitality. They do not serve you in creating a peaceful, thriving world in which you, your children, and your animals can live. They are not true. They are not real. They are based in fear and they are harming you. Just let them go without a second thought. Know that you are fully supported by The Light in all ways, right here and right now. You are safe.

Once you feel that you have completed the releasing process, you can feel peace in knowing that the low-vibrational energies have been cleared away for good. Breathe in joy, breathe in light, breathe in love, and say aloud the new, empowering beliefs that you have written down, knowing that they are true. Know that as you say each one, you are grounding it within your being and making it so. Once you have said them all, say the following, and your Higher Self and Guides will support you in grounding them: "All transformations in my highest good are and will continue to be grounded on all levels of my being, in my highest good. It is so."

This is important work. Remember that the low vibrations you hold within yourself on any level will lower your vibrational state.

CHAPTER FOUR

REAL-LIFE
APPLICATION

Before you can apply all of this to everyday life, you need to know about grounding and using your intuition.

Grounding

Grounding is to be connected through intention and energy both to your physical body and to the vibrational space that you need, in your highest good. Grounding techniques are different for different people. Most empaths simply cannot ground directly into Earth. Therefore, intend to ground your energy where you need it, in your highest good. You do not have to know where this is, just intend it, because there is a wise part of your energy that knows. There are many spiritual techniques that teach people to ground themselves by imagining roots growing from their feet into the Earth, or by somehow pushing their energy into the Earth. Once again, to be clear, this is not suited for empaths.

Grounding is essential for empaths. But a lot of the ways that many people talk about it are incomplete or not applicable in helpful ways to very sensitive, empathic people. Consider it this way:

Imagine that you are going for a drive in your car. It is a hot day, and you are feeling comfortable in the perfectly adjusted temperature of the air conditioning. As you listen to your favorite music, you know that you are safe and protected inside of your car, and you can relax and focus upon your ride.

Now imagine that one leg is hanging outside of the car, letting in the hot air and chemicals from other vehicles' exhaust. Your leg is dragging along the road while feeling every bump, banging against other cars as they go by, and even being run over a few times. Your leg has no protection against the harshness of road travel when it is not inside of the car. Even your car itself is causing you to feel pain as the door slams into your leg over and over again. You cannot concentrate on driving well because you are so distracted by the pain and confusion that is happening to you. This is what it feels like to be ungrounded—bombarded by harmful energies at every turn, feeling beaten up and afraid of what is next to come. Many sensitive, empathic kids and adults feel like this because they are not grounded. If this was what you were experiencing every day, you would end up with a psychiatric diagnosis like so many of them do.

Now, conceptualize in the above example that the car is your body, and you are your soul energy. **When your energy is not connected to and present where your body is located, you are ungrounded.** Imagine that the outside of the car (your body) is your energy field, surrounding you, keeping you safe. With the door open (your personal boundaries not strong) and your energy not fully present inside, you are setting yourself up for pain, illness, and struggle on all levels. This is why it is so imperative to be present, and to allow yourself to be connected to your body.

Your ability to remain grounded is affected by the thoughts and actions you take each day. Think of the car example again. If your car is full of trash, moldy fast food containers, cola bottles, cigarette butts, and dirt, is this a place where you would want to stick around to be fully present to enjoy a nice ride? Would your children want to be riding in a car of this kind of condition? To honor yourself, you have to create a space within your body and your home (where your body lives) that feels good to your energy, so that you want to be there. Consuming toxic food additives, preservatives, pesticides, herbicides, GMOs, antibiotics, hormones, sugar, chemicals, and cigarettes fills your cells with what is akin to a brown sludge. Their natural vitality is stifled by the toxic elements that are bombarding them each day. And therefore, **your beautiful light-energy will choose not to be present with your body. When this occurs, grounding becomes** *extremely* **difficult.**

For empaths, it is vital to keep your body clean so that it will function to its highest capacity, as designed. For many, this involves some degree of initial detoxification, and for all, continued maintenance. Our world is polluted with chemicals, toxins, emotional and physical violence, and the pain of people causing harm to others and the planet because they believe they are separate. Empaths feel and sense all of this. So you have to keep as many harmful elements away from yourself as possible, starting with what you expose your body to every day.

Keep in mind that synergistic combinations of toxic chemicals in vaccinations, medications, and chemicals on and in food and water have different effects for different people. For anyone whose health has been very adversely affected, the focus upon detoxification—while also supporting the body through proper nutrition—is essential. Once this is accomplished, you can choose to bring your energy present with your body, and to allow yourself to ground. This grounding results in connection so that you can interact with other people, focus and concentrate on your tasks, feel peaceful, and be healthy.

If you want to cover the symptoms of toxicity and provide an inauthentic form of grounding either for yourself or your kids, see a doctor for some medication. If you want to get to the heart of the issues affecting your or their inabilities to thrive, focus upon doing what you need to do to really get grounded. This involves different action steps for different people, but the goal of grounding is the same.

Make your body a safe space for your soul to live. Make your home a safe space for your soul to live with your body.

All of the tools I have shared help you to be grounded. Your energy needs to feel safe to be here fully. When toxins on all of these levels are removed and high vibrational beliefs and experiences are added into your space, your energy can ground. Empaths are highly sensitive people. We need things to be done a different way, but this is the way of the future. If these toxins are not removed from this planet, human beings will destroy life here. Remember your gift and implement it in your life as fully as possible. Then you will be helping yourself and everyone else as well.

Using Empathic Intuition to Receive Answers

As an empath, you have a special access to receive intuitive guidance that those who are not able to feel as much do not. Here is a simple yet important tool for determining what is in your best interest to eat and receiving answers to other questions about *your own self.* Because many empaths are very sensitive to foods, it is often a good idea to consult with your intuition before eating. It is important to be grounded when directly consulting your intuition. Once you have brought your energy present, and then cleared and grounded yourself, sit or stand quietly and breathe with the intention of tuning into your own being. As an empath, you can pick up on many different energies. Tune yourself, as if with a radio dial, to your own energy by saying, "I tune to my own energy now." Ask your energy to show you what "yes" feels like, and then what "no" feels like. Ask again for verification. Now, every time you ask, you will pay attention to these sensations within yourself as messages of "yes" or "no." Make sure to get present, clear, and grounded first, or your answers will be distorted.

Real-Life Examples

Because I am an extremely highly sensitive empath, I am going to share with you some personal experiences in which I have used my knowledge of energy and empathic sensitivity to help myself effectively. Please keep in mind that, before I knew about all of this, I was truly struggling. If I had allowed myself to be diagnosed, I am positive I would have been labeled with some kind of mental health condition such as bipolar disorder. Additionally, I was always physically feeling ill in some way, with headaches and migraines, sore throats, respiratory infections, stomach aches and digestive problems, or pelvic pain. However, I pushed through it all, determined to find another way to experience my life. Once I stopped searching for reasons and labels, and I dealt head-on with the energy itself, everything changed for me for the better. And my precious empathic son, who had also been suffering, was able to be healthy, happy, successful, and thriving once he employed the techniques and concepts as well.

STORY #1

The Grocery Store

Grocery stores can be an especially unpleasant place for empaths and those with high sensitivity. Think about all of that food, much of it highly processed and laced with chemicals of all kinds. People are allergic and sensitive to not only foods, but to the chemicals used in processing, growing, and producing foods. Usually there are more products in grocery stores than just foods, and they host a slew of chemicals, including household cleaners, body products, and cosmetics. Top it all off with fluorescent lighting and possibly pumped-in, chemical fragrances, and you have a really toxic energetic space. As an empath walking into this space, you have to be aware of all of that toxic energy so you can protect yourself and maintain your boundaries.

Here is something that I experienced in a large grocery store when I was in the middle of my intensive journey of healing and awakening:

I was shopping in the store and had to go to the aisle where the household cleaners and chemicals were. The large liquor section was right behind me. Quite suddenly, I felt as if I was going to start crying. This feeling was accompanied by nausea and a sense that I wanted to cover my ears and start screaming. Thankfully, I had my wits about me, so I was able to call out in my mind and ask for help from The Light. I did not have the grounding tools that I do now, so my surrender and trust were vital to my making it out of this situation with my pride intact. At this point, I still felt that there was something very wrong with me for having experiences like this, but I also knew more about energy, and I realized that I was reacting to something in my space. The severe feelings quieted and I regained my composure and moved swiftly out of the store.

Now, if something like this has ever happened to you or your child, you probably know how easy it is to judge yourself. You see everyone else shopping quietly while you are suffering inside and possibly showing it on the outside as well. It is so easy to ask, "Why me? What is wrong with me?" I know. However, we have to remember not to do this. There is nothing wrong with you or your child. If you have the gift of being an empath, you are going to feel stuff. And if you are in a place where there is a lot of low-vibrational, toxic energy, you are going to feel the dissonance of that.

Here is how I handle going to the grocery store today. First of all, 99 percent of the trips I make are to small, locally run, natural and organic food stores. These establishments also carry non-toxic household cleaners, body products, and cosmetics. I make sure that I am thoroughly grounded before entering, and I usually wear earplugs to block out the extra sounds from the music and people talking over loud speakers, so that my body will have less stimulation to process. This helps me to remain grounded. I carry my crystals with me and always surround myself with white and colored light. I take my list, get what I need, and get out of there. Then I immediately clear the food and anything I have purchased, and clear and ground myself. Doing all of this prevents any unpleasant reactions and experiences. The extra efforts are all worth it. I can now visit these types of stores often during the week with no problems.

On the occasion when I need to go into a regular, large grocery store, I do the same things, but I also have to really engage my mental level. I tell myself to remain focused upon finding what I have come to buy and to ignore absolutely everything else. What I do not pay attention to cannot harm me. If I go into the energy of it, then I have invited it into my space and have to deal with that. For example, if I have gone into the store to buy some organic spinach, I will not spend any time at all even looking at the other produce that is non-organic. I will not stop and examine or think about items in the bakery, cosmetics, or absolutely anything else. I do not pay attention to it. I treat it as if it does not exist. If I need to go down the cleaning aisle to buy a mop, I ignore—to the very best of my ability—all of the chemicals there. I just do not give them any importance. Try it, it works. And I do not go into these stores more than once a week.

So now, am I crazy and unstable? No, I feel fine going to the store, and all is well. As with anything else, I had to find ways to live in a world that is not currently designed for highly sensitive people like me.

STORY #2

Social Networking

Any empath who uses Facebook or any type of social networking online needs to be very aware. There was a period of time when I was using a social networking site to attempt to connect with like-minded people. It was very different from Facebook in that most of the people there were directly going through or had gone through their own, personal awakening journeys. Therefore, there were hundreds and thousands of people shifting their energy, writing all about it, and offering advice to each other online. When I would go onto the site, I would feel a very uncomfortable lump in my throat. I tried to ignore it for a few months until I started feeling the lump as soon as I logged in. It took me such a long time to get the message that this was not a good place for me to be spending my time. There was just too much energy floating around there that needed to be cleared away and was not being taken care of. I had to leave. Once I did, there was no more lump in my throat.

I want to share with you that, as I was proofreading the last paragraph, I felt the lump in my throat come back! So here is what I did: First, I reminded myself that the painful lump feeling is a message to me—do not return to that website! Then, I asked for assistance from, with, and within The Light, to cut the ties of entanglement to anything negative or harmful, and to clear the energy. I re-cleared and grounded myself. Because I still felt the discomfort, I made a special request of The Light to keep all low vibrations away from me on all levels of my being. Despite doing all of this, whenever I read this section for some time, I still felt the sensation. Again, I take it as a message to remember the experiences I had there and not to repeat them.

Similarly, Facebook and sites like it can really affect empaths. People post all kinds of things, and some it can be quite negative. Also, I have seen a lot of well-intentioned spiritually minded people post information that is just not authentic and aligned with The Light. All of this is energy, and if it is not pure and light, it is going to feel dissonant to an empath. If you are using Facebook regularly and are having any types of pains, ill health, or depression, I recommend that you completely stop using it. Also, if you do use it—which I still do sometimes—make absolutely sure that you thoroughly clear and ground yourself immediately afterward. This will assure that you are no longer connected to any of the energy on there.

Empathic Kids and School

When my son was in Kindergarten through second grade, we did not have the knowledge or tools that we do today. I knew that he was highly sensitive and I was taking him to see a lot of different healers. However, he did not have tools of his own to use when he was away from home on his own at school. The results of this were that every day when he would come home, he would spend one to two hours crying hysterically. **Every day.** He also got sick and had respiratory allergies very often.

When we would talk about what could be upsetting him so much, he would always draw reference to children at school who were struggling. He would go on and on about how someone could not control themselves and kept getting in trouble with the teacher. Or how someone was mean to someone else and he had been witness to it. The more he learned about how food affects the body, he more upset he would be about the junk foods that he saw the other children eating at school. And no matter how much I talked to him about maintaining his own boundaries and how everyone is on their own path, he still continued to be so upset and to cry each and every day.

It was not until I learned about empathic sensitivity

that things started to make more sense. He could feel very deeply those children's pain. He could feel when someone was bullied as if it had happened to him. He could feel the imbalances within the children that were causing them to act out and to struggle and get in trouble. He could feel everything, and he was doing everything in his power not to cry at school, so that by the time he got home, it all had to come out.

Once I gave him specific tools to clear and ground himself, the crying stopped. Once I taught him about how empathic sensitivity works, he could understand that none of the unpleasant things he was feeling had anything to do directly with him. He was okay, even if someone was feeling like they were not. This awareness changed his life and he continues to be successful and happy out in the world today, even as sensitive as he is.

STORY #4

The Phantom Pains

Empaths feel stuff, and sometimes it comes on very suddenly. Once I had gained awareness and I began using tools for myself, I would go through my days feeling mostly stable and good. However, there continued to be a period of time whenever my husband would come home when I would collapse immediately in terrible pain; sometimes I would start crying, too. He thought that it was about him personally, which created some problems for us for a while. However, finally, I realized that it had nothing to do directly with him. It was the energy he was bringing home with him from his day at work that he had failed to clear away. Once I explained this to him and showed him how to clear himself, the painful episodes completely stopped for me. Yes, it was that instantaneous.

So was there something wrong with me because I felt the pain he was carrying around with him? Absolutely not! This is exactly how being an empath is a gift to all those around you. Now, my husband's energy remains clear, so he can feel better overall as well.

I used to get random, shooting pains all the time. I would wonder, "What is wrong with me now?" Of course, there was nothing wrong with me, but I did not know that then. So I would take ibuprofen or acetaminophen and just feel self-pity about it. Now, however, I immediately recognize that whatever is causing the pain is not me or mine, and neither is the pain itself. In the same instant, I make the decision to clear all low vibrations away from myself. I also do this for hives, which is another way that you may find yourself reacting to low-vibrational energies. Usually, within minutes the issues are resolved.

There is nothing wrong with me because I feel the icky stuff that exists in this world. I am sure of this today. I hope that you will come to this place of knowing within yourself, so that you can do what you need to do to thrive in honoring ways.

The Awareness Empaths Need for Thriving

In closing, please recall the most important pieces of information for empaths to live healthy, thriving lives:

1. If it does not feel good, it is not yours.

2. LET GO of what is not yours.

3. Clear away what you have let go of.

4. Remove yourself from toxic experiences on all levels and maintain awareness of your own boundaries.

5. Take care of your body and energy on all levels in the most honoring ways possible for yourself.

And last, but not least: **You are NOT crazy or mentally ill because you FEEL!**

RESOURCES

The Empathic Sensitivity Blog: www.empathicsensitivity.com

The Foundations System: Working with Multidimensional Energy for Thriving by Janice Carlin, Ph.D.

The Angel Therapy Handbook by Doreen Virtue, Ph.D. (Hay House: 2012)

About the Author

Janice Carlin, Ph.D. is an author, intuitive channel, teacher, and mom. She has a master's degree in Music: Conducting, and a Ph.D. in Holistic Natural Health and Nutrition. She is a certified practitioner of Natural Health, Holistic Nutrition, and Holographic Sound Healing.

It is Janice's passion to empower people to live thriving lives in natural ways and to heal themselves and their children. Janice has deep experiential knowledge about the challenges of living on planet Earth as a highly sensitive empath. She walks her talk through her maintenance of a pure, clean diet and lifestyle. The channeled messages she shares cut through limiting beliefs to make room for people to be able to live with vitality, to heal themselves and their children, and to better our world. She is committed to sharing only that which is from, with, and within The Light in the highest benefit of all.

Janice uniquely bridges the gap between science and spirituality, teaching ways that sensitive people can work effectively with multidimensional energy to help themselves and their sensitive children to thrive. She channeled and developed a revolutionary and accessible way for people to work effectively with multidimensional energy for healing, clearing, and manifestation called The Foundations System. In it, she provides the three keys for being empowered to thrive, which are: Knowing who you really are on a soul level, or your Soul Energy Type; knowing how energy works; and knowing how to work with energy effectively and in alignment with The Light for the highest benefit of all. She also teaches about Soul Energy Types to assist people in remembering their true purpose and mission for incarnating, as well as their personal, unique needs for being able to thrive.

Janice is also the author of *The Foundations System, Be Free,* and *Toward Ascension.*

She can be found online at:

http://www.empoweredthriving.com/